Sarden's Practical Guide: How to Start Homeschooling

JUDY SARDEN

JUDY SARDEN

Copyright © 2018 Judy Sarden

All rights reserved.

No part of this book may be reproduced, or stored in a retrieval system, or transmitted in any form or by any means, electronic, mechanical, photocopying, recording, or otherwise, without express permission of the publisher.

Published by Sarden Publishing

www.thesardens.com

ISBN: 0999743600
ISBN-13: 978-0999743607

JUDY SARDEN

To the big guy and the small people whose love and support allowed me to follow a dream.

JUDY SARDEN

CONTENTS

Introduction   i

Part I How To Get Your Homeschool Started

1. Research Your State Homeschool Laws   5
2. Decide When to Take Your Kids Out of School   15
3. Determine What Your School Will Look Like   23
4. Choosing Curriculum   35
5. Make an Assessment Before You Begin Homeschooling   47
6. Location of Your Homeschool   55
7. Setting a Schedule   59

Part II Advice and Encouragement

8. You Do Have the Patience to Homeschool   67
9. Don't Let Homeschooling Get in the Way of Learning   75
10. De-schooling   81
11. Realize Much of Your Planning Will Be In Vain   87
12. Remember to Enjoy Your Children   91
13. Incorporate Learning Into Your Daily Life   97
14. Working While Homeschooling   103
15. Socialization   109

Acknowledgments   115

JUDY SARDEN

INTRODUCTION

This *Sarden's Practical Guide: How to Start Homeschooling* is intended to be short, sweet and to the point. When I was considering homeschooling, I did a ton of research. I bought several homeschooling books. The problem is, most of the books were long and contained more information than I could digest.

Reading a long book is great when you have a year to plan your homeschool starting point. However, over the years that I've been homeschooling I have seen that there is a real need for a short, practical, "how to" guide to begin homeschooling.

I have spoken to many parents who needed to withdraw their children from school immediately. These parents clearly do not have the time to read multiple, lengthy books on homeschooling.

Similarly, parents who are currently homeschooling may be struggling with their homeschool situation and may need help figuring out how to reboot.

Many parents need step by step instructions in order to get up and running quickly, and the lengthy, sometimes theoretical, books on homeschooling are simply insufficient for those parents.

My hope is that this *Guide* is helpful for parents who are considering homeschooling, who have decided to homeschool but do not know where to start, and for those parents who are already homeschooling but need to reboot or consider other options.

JUDY SARDEN

PART I

HOW TO GET YOUR HOMESCHOOL STARTED

JUDY SARDEN

"There is no school equal to a decent home and no teacher equal to a virtuous parent."

Mahatma Ghandi

JUDY SARDEN

1

RESEARCH YOUR STATE HOMESCHOOL LAWS

Researching the home education laws for your state is probably the most important step to complete after making the decision to homeschool your children. Homeschool laws vary by state and can be quite complex. They can also change from year to year, so it's always a good idea to revisit the laws at the beginning of each school year.

There are several layers of home education laws that you'll need to understand. Overall, they fall into 5 categories.

Does Your State Allow Homeschooling

The good news is that homeschooling is allowed in every state. The trick is to finding out where your homeschool laws are located.

In most cases you would look under your state's education laws. You could look at your state department of education or even your local school district's website in order to find the information. In most cases, your state will have a specific homeschooling statute. However, if your state does not have a statute that is obvious, you should locate a homeschooling organization in your state or contact your local board of education.

If you do end up contacting your local board of education, be prepared for some negativity as regards to taking your children out of school and homeschooling them. If this happens, do not to be discouraged. Simply ask for the information and then carry on with your research.

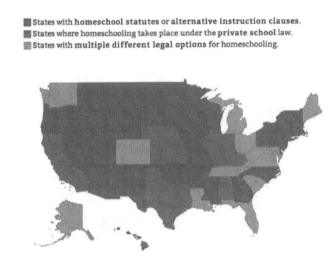

Figure 1 www.responsiblehomeschooling.org

Notification Requirements

Some states require no notice of intent to homeschool. In those states, parents owe no notification to the zoned school, the local board of education or the state board of education. Other states' notification requirements require one time notice, while others require annual notification.

Those states that require notification may require different types of notification for different homeschool setups. For example, if families are required to associate with an umbrella school, the family may not have to notify education officials because that responsibility falls on the umbrella school.

In other situations, a child may not be considered a homeschooler so no notification is required at all. An example of this would be an online public or private school or a hybrid homeschool.

After you have determined whether you must provide notice, you must comply with the notice requirement content. Notice content can range from a short description of the name, age and grade of the child to providing the year's lesson plan and the child's birth certificate. Be sure to follow these requirements exactly.

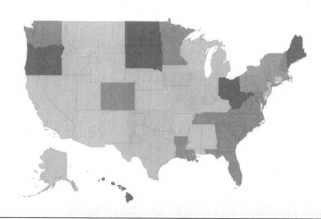

Figure 2 www.responsiblehomeschooling.org

Notification by State

No Notification: AK, CT, ID, IA, IL, IN, MI, MO, NJ, OK, TX

One Time Notification: AL, AZ, FL, HI, KS, ME, NC, NV, OR, UT

Annual Notification: AR, CA, CO, DE, GA, KY, LA, MD, MA, MN, MS, MT, NE, NY, NM, NY, ND, OH, PA, RI, SC, SD, TN, VT, VA, WA, WV, WI, WY

Parent Qualifications

In most cases, a parent need only possess a high school diploma or equivalent in order to homeschool their children.

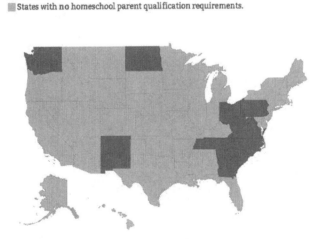

Figure 3 www.responsiblehomeschooling.org

Instructional Requirements:

States' instructional requirements are all over the place. Some states require certain subjects be taught, others require a set number of instructional hours or days per school year, while other states have both subject and instructional hour requirements. Then there are some states that have no instructional requirements at all.

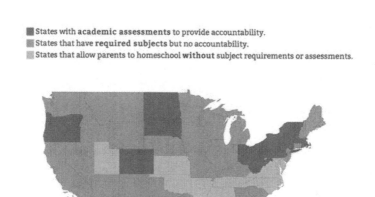

Figure 4 www.responsiblehomeschooling.org

Testing and Assessment

In addition to subject matter and instructional time requirements, many states will have assessment or testing requirements. Testing and assessment requirements can range from testing every few years using the test of your choice to annual assessments using designated tests. Additionally, some states only require you to keep the test results in your files, while others require the results be turned in to an education official.

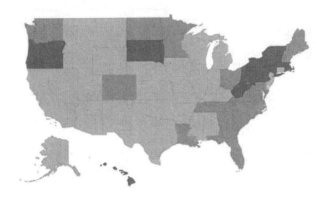

Figure 5 www.responsiblehomeschooling.org

For many parents, navigating homeschool laws can feel like a daunting task and the fear of running afoul of the laws can sometimes prevent parents from taking the plunge.

CHAPTER TAKEAWAY

I encourage parents to resist the fear of homeschool laws. A careful read of the laws is all that is necessary to understand them. You can spend one day familiarizing yourself with the state legal requirements and then you're done. Here is what you need to do:

1. Visit your state's Department of Education website and search for "home education" and "homeschool." There, you should find everything you need to know about the home

education laws.

2. Do a general Google search for "[your state] homeschool laws." This should provide additional sources that you can read to acquaint yourself with your state's homeschool laws. Just be sure that your sources are valid, up to date, and don't conflict with the requirements you read on the Department of Education website.

3. From your research, make a list of what you need to do, e.g., notify the local school, submit your intent to homeschool, and list any subject or instructional time requirements.

4. Visit www.thesardens.com/howtohomeschoolbook for colorized versions of the map and more homeschool legal requirement resources. Visit www.responsiblehomeschooling for more information about proposed homeschooling legislation.

"The home is the first and most effective place to learn the lessons of life: truth, honor, virtue, self-control, the value of education, honest work, and the purpose and privilege of life."

David O. McKay

2

DECIDE WHEN TO TAKE YOUR KIDS OUT OF SCHOOL

Now that you understand your state legal requirements, you can decide on a start date. Many parents decide sometime during the school year that they will begin homeschooling the following school year. With homeschooling becoming more mainstreamed, however, a growing number of parents are deciding mid-year to withdraw their kids from school and begin homeschooling. These situations are very different so we will address them separately.

Beginning at the start of the school year

In several states, parents are allowed to set the school calendar for their home school. But for the sake of this discussion, we will assume that the beginning of the school year is sometime in August. This is probably the easiest time of year to begin homeschooling because this is the time when all the other kids return to school.

If you know ahead of time that you're planning to begin your school year at the same time the brick-and-mortar schools start, you'll have the flexibility to do a few things.

First, you'll have the opportunity to look for curricula, perhaps attend a homeschool convention, and really get a sense of the shape you want your homeschool to take.

Second, this is probably the best time of year to start because you will feel less pressure to quickly get up and going than you would if you pulled your child out to the middle of the school year. Since your child will have had her summer break, you'll have less need to engage in de-schooling, as covered in Chapter 10.

Third, starting your homeschool at the beginning of the typical school year will give you the summer months to ensure that you have researched and followed all of your state and local homeschooling requirement. Unless required by your state and local laws, you will not have to formally withdraw your child from school, thereby avoiding any uncomfortable conversations with the school administration.

Finally, having the summer to prepare yourself and your child for homeschooling gives everyone a chance to ease into the new schooling arrangement.

Beginning at a random time during the school year

More and more, I talk to parents who have reached their limit with their child's school and on, say, a Tuesday afternoon in November, they decide that their child will not be attending the school anymore and that they are going to begin homeschooling.

This has to be one of the scariest and most intimidating prospects for a new homeschooling parent. Indeed, it is this parent who inspired me to write this book. If you are that parent, let me first encourage you to take a breath and know that everything will be okay. Here is what you should do if you are pulling your child out in the middle of the school year:

1. Do a search of your state and local laws. This is the most important step in the process of removing your child from school. Everyone has heard horror stories of parents getting in trouble with child services. The best way to avoid such a situation is to make sure you are following state laws.
2. Follow the steps for withdrawing your child as set forth by your state Department of Education and your local board of education. This information should be readily available on the respective websites. Go to your state Department of Education website and type: "homeschool," or "homeschooling," in the search bar. Likewise for your local board of education website. Do these things before you speak to your school representatives as they will likely try to dissuade you from removing your child from school.
3. Look for state homeschooling associations. For example, if you live in North Carolina, you would Google: North Carolina Homeschool Association. These websites and representatives in these organizations can often help fill in the gaps if you have any questions about your state homeschool requirements.
4. Once you understand what your requirements and rights are within your state, follow all the necessary steps and withdraw your child from school.
5. After you have withdrawn your child from school, the first thing you'll need to do is read Chapter 10 about de-schooling. If you pulled your child from school in the middle of the school year, it is likely because of deteriorated social or academic issues. In many cases, these children need academic support and a self-esteem boost. This is what the de-schooling period is for.
6. During your de-schooling time, you'll want to get a sense of where your child is academically. You'll get a sense of what his interests are and you may begin to gain insight into his

learning style. You will aquire this knowledge of your child through the de-schooling process and through light academic assignments that are mostly geared towards collecting this information, rather than pushing ahead academically.
7. The reason this information is important is because you will then use it to find curricula. You'll notice that finding curricula is pretty far down on the list of things to do when pulling one's children from school. That is because the curricula you use is really secondary to making sure you follow the laws and learning about what your child's needs are. What I do not recommend is simply rushing out and purchasing a curriculum - any curriculum - and trying to replicate school at home beginning on day one.

Whether you decide to begin your homeschool year in August or in the middle of the school year, you are now ready for your next step - deciding what your homeschool is going to look like. Notice we haven't gotten to choosing a curriculum yet!

CHAPTER TAKEAWAY

Do not be discouraged nor frightened of taking the plunge and homeschooling. Whether you are starting at the beginning of the year or whether you are starting in the middle of the school year, you can do it!

1. Decide when you are going to begin homeschooling your children. Your start date will depend on what is best for your child and your family.
2. Planning to begin your homeschool journey at the beginning of the school year is probably the easiest way to begin homeschooling because you will have had, at a

minimum, the summer to prepare both yourself and your child.
3. Beginning your homeschool journey in the middle of the school year *is* doable! It simply requires a slightly different approach than beginning in August.

JUDY SARDEN

"Knowledge which is acquired under compulsion has no hold on the mind."

Plato

3

DETERMINE WHAT YOUR SCHOOL WILL LOOK LIKE

Homeschooling can take many forms. When most people think about homeschooling, they think about a parent leading all learning activities, similar to the way a teacher would in a school setting. But homeschooling doesn't have to look like that at all. Below I'll discuss some options.

Public School at Home

Most states have some form of school at home. In Georgia, it's called Georgia Cyber Academy. Although originally intended for children who can't attend the brick and mortar school for medical or other reasons, parents can enroll their children if they prefer facilitating their child's learning at home.

This option works great for the parent who may be working full time from home or a parent with an older child who can be left at home to do his work while the parent works outside the home. This is also a great option if the parent works outside the home but can leave a younger child with a family member or sitter.

How it Works

Once you sign up for public school at home, you'll typically be given all the curriculum materials you'll need, just like you would if your child attended public school. The good news is that, with this option *you* are not the teacher.

Your child will typically take all classes online, with either a live teacher or with a pre-recorded lesson. All teaching and assignments will be taken care of by your child's assigned teacher(s). As the facilitator, you or a person who is with your child during the day, simply have to ensure that your child attends "class" at the appointed time.

Many public school at home options will include a "social" aspect where the program administrators will organize field trips and other outings for the at-home kids. These outings provide kids with the chance to see their "class mates," and sometimes their teachers, face to face.

I recommend public school at home for anyone who is planning on returning their children to public school. Public school at home is also good for those whose children are having difficulty keeping up in school and who really need one-on-one attention. I also recommend school at home for those who need to pull their children out immediately, but have no plan for how they are going to homeschool. By using school at home as a temporary solution while you figure it out, you can keep your child "in school" without stressing yourself out while you figure it out.

One of the strengths of public school at home is that you can be sure that your child is being exposed to all that is required by your state. You are not required to teach. You are not required to keep track of grades. You are not required to deal with transcripts. For those parents who experienced anxiety at the thought of having to teach their own children, public school at home can be a wonderful middleground between full-blown homeschooling and keeping your child in a brick-and-mortar public school.

I do not recommend public school at home, however, for parents who want a more relaxed form of homeschooling. One of the drawbacks of public school at home is that it *is* "public school at home." What that means is that you are still on the school's schedule. You are still expected to show up to class at the times and during the times dictated by the school-at-home provider. Another drawback to school at home is that a good portion of the work is done on a computer. For children who do not do well in front of a computer or with an excessive amount of screen time, this can be a problem.

Another drawback to public school at home is that you may be restricted from participating in local "true homeschool" activities because your children must be online during the times that other homeschool activities are taking place. In my own experience, most people who are trying to implement a traditional homeschool find public school at home very restrictive. Whether public school at home works for you and your family will be dependent upon your goals for educating your child as well as your family circumstances.

Private, Online Schools

Online private schools offer another option for homeschooling your children. Similar to public school at home, much of the instruction takes place via computer. One of the major differences between online private school and public school at home is that private online schools are not free whereas public school at home is generally free or extremely low cost.

With a private online school, you will receive all of the required books and learning materials from the school, as well as have online teachers that do the actual teaching. Similar to public school at home, the parent is not required to do any teaching, keep track of grades, or keep transcripts. Many online private schools are also accredited and can offer parents an official transcript.

One of the benefits of private online schools, as opposed to public school at home, is that private online schools typically offer more flexibility than public school at home. Many online private schools will allow a student to work at his or her own pace. Depending on the age of the student, private online schools also tend to offer more electives and more flexibility with regard to outside classes than a public school at home program.

Online private schools are available for both secular and religious-based homeschoolers. If it is important for a family to incorporate Christian teachings in their home school, a private online school will be a better choice over public school at home.

Because online private schools tend to be more flexible, a child has greater opportunity to participate in local homeschool co-op and enrichment programs. In fact, in some cases, the local homeschool program can augment the coursework of the private online school.

Another benefit of the private online school is that they better accommodate children who are working or who are highly talented. For example, working actors, gifted children, professional or student athletes can often be found participating in online private schools.

The biggest drawback of private online school over public school at home is, of course, the cost. Private online school can run from several hundred dollars a semester to a few thousand dollars per semester. So while you do benefit from a greater level of flexibility with a private online school, that flexibility does come at a cost.

Hybrid Schools

Moving along the flexibility continuum, the next type of homeschooling is a hybrid school. With a hybrid school, students will typically attend a brick-and-mortar school two to three days per week. The remaining days are spent at home. During the days that the student attends the brick-and-mortar school, tests are given, assignments are issued, and any necessary teaching takes place. On the days when the student is at home, the parent acts as a facilitator to assist the student in completing assigned work.

A hybrid school offers a wonderful balance between a total school- at-home approach and a full-blown traditional homeschooling. First, the hybrid school is responsible for keeping transcripts, testing and any other requirement as per the state. Furthermore, the parent is still not the teacher; rather, the parent is a facilitator. If the student has questions or needs additional assistance, there are teachers at the hybrid school who can help if the subject matter is beyond the parent.

On the other hand, having two to three days per week at home, the student and parents can enjoy a homeschool-like flexibility that is missing with a public school at home or even a private online school.

Using a hybrid school allows students to participate in local homeschool activities, while still having a more formal school environment; complete with experiencing a classroom setting, grades and in most cases, sports and afterschool activities.

For many families, the hybrid school is the perfect solution for the parent who still wants or needs to work part time, while still allowing them to achieve the goal of homeschooling their children. It is also a great solution for parents who want their children to experience a homeschool environment but the parent does not feel comfortable or confident yet to take on the task of being the teacher, the parent, the administrator, and all the other roles that come with a traditional homeschooling set up.

One of the drawbacks to a hybrid homeschool as compared to public school at home is that this is another option that can run a family hundreds of dollars, to thousands of dollars, per year. In addition, most hybrid home schools require parents to purchase all books and necessary supplies. And many hybrid home schools require some kind of uniform. While hybrid homeschools are typically significantly less expensive than a full-time private school, they will always cost a family more per child than if the children were attending a public school at home.

Traditionally, hybrid home schools have been operated by churches or religious organizations. This works well for parents who are looking for a religious-based homeschool program. Recently, however, more secular hybrid home schools are opening for those families who are not looking for a religious-based education. If you live in a large metropolitan area, you are more likely to find a secular-based hybrid homeschool.

I highly recommend a hybrid homeschool to families where the homeschooling parent needs or wants to work but who also wants to provide a homeschooling experience for their children. I also recommend a hybrid homeschool for families whose children enjoy a formal brick-and-mortar school environment but to also need the flexibility of being at home. Hybrid home schools really are the best of both worlds as they allow older students to participate in the same types of clubs and sporting activities that a typical private school would offer.

And while there will be a cost involved in a hybrid homeschool arrangement, if your children participate in extracurricular activities, you may find that it is cheaper to send them to a hybrid homeschool where the activities are included in the cost of tuition versus paying for each activity separately.

Traditional Homeschooling

If you begin your homeschooling journey using one of the above methods, you may eventually want to consider transitioning to a traditional homeschool. While many people will continue with one of the above methods of homeschooling, many families will choose to move to traditional homeschooling. And I know many families that jumped straight into traditional homeschooling.

With traditional homeschooling, the homeschooling parent and, to an extent, the child, direct the learning at home. This method of homeschooling is nearly as varied as the number of families that are homeschooling. For example, some families will create a school at home environment while still selecting all curricula and managing all the academics, while others will take more of an unschooling approach, where the at home learning is mostly directed by the child.

One's method of implementing traditional homeschooling is totally dependent upon the needs and beliefs of each homeschooling family. For example, I have always been a traditional homeschooler. I chose all of my curricula and I have always been my children's primary teacher. I set the schedule for what we are going to do every day and I create all the requirements for their academic work. While we do have a full set of curricula and academic resources, I have evolved from a very traditional school at home philosophy to a more eclectic, flexible, work-school-around-life approach.

Because my children are getting older, I think it is important that they learn many life skills in addition to their academic work. And so while I do place an emphasis on academics, I place an equal emphasis on acquiring life skills and learning how to function in the real world. If you're interested in what this looks like, you may visit my website at www.thesardens.com and look at my Day in a Homeschool Life Posts.

The best reason for engaging in traditional homeschooling is that it allows you to be 100% flexible. Because you are generally not accountable to anyone but yourself and your family, you have great freedom in directing your children's education, they have great freedom in taking control of their own education, and you can organize your school around your family life. This is especially important for a parent of older children who have to homeschool say, in the evenings, because the parent works a full-time job during the day.

Another benefit of traditional homeschooling is that you can pick and choose curricula for each individual subject separately as opposed to having to work with a one-size-fits-all curriculum like you would if you used one of the other homeschooling methods.

The biggest drawback to traditional homeschooling is that it takes a lot of work from the parent. If both parents work outside the home or are otherwise short on time, I would not recommend traditional homeschooling. Traditional homeschooling requires much time in advanced planning and, since you are your child's primary instructor, it can take up a significant amount of time during your day. If you cannot consistently dedicate a great number of hours during the week in planning and implementing a traditional homeschool curriculum, I would recommend going with one of the other types of homeschool.

The other drawback to traditional homeschooling is the lack of accountability. You are accountable to yourself and to your children but you do not have the day-to-day accountability that you would have from an online or hybrid school. So when you're looking at homeschooling methods, you really have to be honest with yourself and decide which type of homeschool will help you to accomplish what you need to accomplish based on your own personality, schedule and work style.

CHAPTER TAKEAWAY

1. When choosing your homeschool type, be sure to take an honest assessment of your own organizational style, your schedule and your child's needs
2. Remember that the awesome thing about homeschooling is that you can always change course if something isn't working out for you or your child!
3. Visit www.thesardens.com/howtohomeschoolbook for a list of online school options.

"Homeschooling and public schooling are as opposite as two sides of a coin. In a homeschooling environment, the teacher need not be certified, but the child MUST learn. In a public school environment, the teacher MUST be certified, but the child need NOT learn."

Gene Royer

4

CHOOSING CURRICULUM

Choosing curriculum is, hands down, the most overwhelming aspect of beginning your homeschool. I always recommend that new homeschoolers visit a homeschool convention, but I have found that many beginners find homeschool conventions to be incredibly overwhelming.

That said homeschooling conferences provide you with an opportunity to talk to curriculum providers, talk to other homeschooling families, and attend workshops that may help you to get a better idea of what homeschooling entails.

When we were thinking about homeschooling, my husband and I attended a conference. The best class we attended was entitled "How to Home Educate Boys." This class was awesome because it helped us to understand how boys think and learn. Without this class, my first year of homeschooling would have been much less pleasant.

Whether you visit a homeschool convention or simply look online, you'll find boxed curricula, single subject curricula and general learning resources that are not intended to be a complete curriculum.

Boxed Curriculum

A boxed curriculum is just that – all of your curriculum needs are purchased from one publisher and it arrives in a box.

I recommend boxed curricula to parents who are wanting to implement a 100% traditional homeschool experience but who are just starting and do not have the time or the confidence to put together a curriculum themselves. This option also works for parents who are working part-time or even full time, but who have figured out a way to manage their time so that they can teach their children.

An example a boxed curriculum would be one where, for one price, you receive all math, reading, science, and elective materials, and sometimes even the readers that go along with the literature and history assignments. With these books, you would typically get a calendar or scheduler that would instruct you on which pages to assign for each day of the week, typically spanning over 36 weeks.

The great benefit of using a boxed curriculum is that someone has gone through and selected all of your books for you and has organized everything. All you have to do is open your schedule and you know exactly what to work on each day. There is no guesswork. Your entire year is planned out for you.

Another benefit of a boxed curriculum is that it gives you total flexibility. For example, many box curricula offer a four or five day option. Homeschool families like to homeschool for four days out of the week, leaving one day as a catch up day, co-op day or as a get outside and do something fun day.

Having a four-day schedule already lined up for you allows you to get all of your schoolwork done and still have time to participate in your other homeschool activities.

Another benefit of the boxed curriculum is that they often come with scripts for implementing some of the curricula. For example, if you do not think that you are good in math, or if you think that you would not know what to say for the literature assignment, you can choose a boxed curriculum that provides you with a script. You simply open your scheduler or planner, see what's on tap for the day, read the script for the designated subject, and then have your child work on the assignment.

Another feature of a boxed curriculum is that they offer customer service. So if you find that there is a subject or something that you're just confused about, you can always email or call someone and have them walk you through it.

If you are a new homeschool parent and you are nervous about "teaching" your children, but you still want to homeschool them and maintain a maximum amount of flexibility, I strongly recommend purchasing a boxed curriculum.

Boxed curricula take the guesswork out of choosing single subject curricula and will help you to feel less overwhelmed. In the grand scheme of things, there are far fewer total boxed curricula than there are single subject curricula. If you plan to attend a homeschool convention, you don't need to get overwhelmed by the numerous individual curriculum choices. Purchasing a boxed curriculum is simply a matter of choosing which company you're going to use to provide you with all of your curriculum needs. All you'll need to do is visit the few booths that offer complete boxed curricula and find one that you like. For a list of popular boxed curricula, visit www.thesardens.com/howtohomeschoolbook.

Often, people who really want the maximum amount of flexibility in their homeschool complain that they cannot find a boxed curriculum that provides everything they need. If you begin using a boxed curriculum and you find that it's not providing everything you need, but it is providing most of what you need, you can always supplement in the areas where you find a deficiency. Finding something to supplement the whole curriculum is far less onerous and intimidating than picking and choosing several subjects from multiple publishers and vendors.

While I cannot over emphasize the benefits of using a boxed curriculum, they do have drawbacks. One of the major drawbacks is upfront cost. A boxed curriculum with schedule and scripts for the parents can run several hundreds of dollars per grade. Many of the items purchased may also be consumables, meaning the material cannot be reused, like workbooks. However, if budget is an issue, I recommend that you think of it like this. If you have multiple children, much of the boxed curriculum can be reused. Indeed, since a box curricula is intended for homeschool families, many of which have multiple children, they tend to be set up in such a way that they can be used with multiple children over several years.

So even if 20% of the box curriculum is made up of consumables, when your next child comes through that grade, you're not having to purchase several hundreds of dollars worth of curriculum, but rather the few workbooks that are necessary to go along with the curriculum that you already have. Therefore, this drawback becomes a benefit if you use the boxed curriculum with multiple children.

Pick and Choose Your Own Curriculum

Finally, you have the option to pick and choose your own curriculum. This can be very overwhelming if you are new to homeschooling. It basically entails choosing which individual curriculum you want to use for each subject – science, math, reading, grammar, spelling, science, and so on. I recommend this method for families that have homeschooled for at least one year. That said, when I began homeschooling I jumped right into this type of homeschooling.

The reason why I chose this type of homeschooling is because I was not looking for a religion based curriculum and found it very difficult to find any of the above mentioned curriculum options that did not have a religious component. Specifically, I was not looking for a science curriculum with a new earth perspective nor was I looking for history curriculum that was biblically based. I could have chosen one of the above curriculum choices and simply replaced the science or history or not included some of the Bible lessons, but instead I chose to put my curriculum together from scratch.

From my own experience, I can say that taking this approach was expensive. It was also extremely time-consuming on my behalf because I had to spend many, many hours researching individual curricula for each subject. In hindsight, I think it would have been better for me to choose a boxed curriculum and then decide what I did and did not like during the year, and then move on to a pick and choose curriculum option.

By using a pick and choose curriculum approach, not only did I have to spend an inordinate amount of time choosing a curriculum for each subject, but I then had to put together a schedule, organize all the lessons, find supplementary material, and then review instructors' manual for each subject in preparation for the day's lessons.

On the other hand, the pick and choose approach gave me an incredible amount of freedom to teach my children. I think that if I used one of the above curriculum approaches, I would have felt less confident about changing things up if they weren't working. I also think I would've felt pressured if I was not keeping up with the schedule and calendar as laid out by the scheduler.

Here's how to find success with the pick and choose curriculum method:

1. You decide what subjects you want to teach for the year
2. Taking each subject separately, research all the available curricula for that subject. When doing this, I suggest that you attend a homeschool convention where you can see, touch and feel the curricula that you are considering using.
3. Purchase your favorite curricula and take time to review everything.
4. Determine how much of each subject you would like to cover over the course of your school year. For example, you may decide that you don't want to cover every chapter.
5. Decide how long you would like to homeschool for the year and then divide your curriculum up into workable chunks. Determine what you need to accomplish each month in order to cover everything by the end of the year.
6. Prepare a rough, high level schedule of what you want to complete each month. If you are a super organized person, go ahead and plan out your entire year. If you're like me, plan out your schedule for the week or if that's not enough for you, plan it out for the month.

I have really enjoyed using this approach as it suits my personality. It has allowed me to be very flexible in my homeschool and it has allowed me to change things up quickly if they were not working. For example, I went through two math programs before I settled on the third. I went through three language arts programs before settling on my fourth. I've gone through numerous science programs before settling on no curriculum at all – we use many science resources but follow no formal text book format. And while I have loosely stayed with my original history curriculum, I supplement so heavily it doesn't really look like a curriculum at all.

Using a pick and choose approach has really allowed me to cater my children's education towards their learning styles and needs.

Coops

Co-ops are generally run by a group of parents that have gotten together to provide academic and enrichment classes for their children. In some cases, the academic classes are taught by co-op parents who have an expertise in the area in which they are teaching. Other co-ops will bring in private school teachers or even university professors to teach some of the classes, particularly for middle and high school math and sciences. Some co-op arrangements allow you to drop your child off and others require parents to stay the entire time to assist with childcare or other duties.

Using co-ops can be a great option for your homeschool regardless of what curriculum method you use. They are great if your child only needs to take one or a few classes to supplement his academic work. For example, I have no intentions of teaching my children geometry. While I was good at math, geometry is an absolute no-go for me. So when the time comes, I will find a co-op that has a geometry class that my kids can take.

If you live in an area that does not have a co-op, I encourage you to start one with other homeschoolers in the area. I really love co-op options for the life skill classes. For example, I've seen co-ops that offer courses in household plumbing, carpentry, basic auto mechanics and other courses. I love it that my homeschooled kids have the opportunity to participate in these kinds of classes.

Enrichment Classes

Enrichment classes are classes that supplement the regular academic coursework. These would include art, music, dance, coding, sewing and even some academic classes. Enrichment classes can be found in local communities or online. Many co-ops offer enrichment classes. And many facilities that offer afterschool and weekend extracurricular classes will also offer homeschool enrichment classes. If you do not have these in your area for homeschoolers, I encourage you to get a group of homeschoolers together and then approach a business to see if they would be willing to offer homeschool enrichment classes.

Many homeschoolers like homeschool enrichment classes because they are filled with other homeschoolers, because they are offered during the middle of the school day and because the classes tend to be much smaller.

My children have enjoyed both homeschool and afterschool enrichment classes and I think there is a benefit to both. They like homeschool enrichment classes because they get to take them with their friends. I like the homeschool enrichment classes because they tend to be smaller and the children get more individualized attention. Because children are taking these classes as part of their academic day, I find that the level of instruction tends to be higher level and more school like than in the afterschool enrichment class. In our experience, the homeschooled students tend to be more engaged and interested in the topic, allowing instructors to go deeper into the subject matter.

On the other hand, afterschool enrichment classes offer a more diverse experience. If the class is performance-based, like dance or theater, I find that the productions and expectations tend to be higher for the afterschool students. For example, when my daughter took musical theater, the homeschool musical theater class met one day a week and held its year-end recital at the studio; whereas the afterschool version of musical theater met three times per week and held its year-end recital at the county Civic Center.

So my personal preference for enrichment classes is for my children to take fine arts classes with the homeschool group but to do sports and performance related activities with an afterschool program.

Online Classes

An almost limitless number of online homeschool classes are offered to homeschooled children. Examples of classes my kids have taken are: art, Minecraft, math, and science. For middle grade and high school students, many of the higher level math, science and language arts classes are offered online.

All you need to do to find these classes is google "homeschool class" or "online homeschool" or "homeschool [subject you are looking for]."

CHAPTER TAKEAWAY

1. Rather than looking at curriculum options as overwhelming, try to rejoice in the fact that you have so many options and that you can choose what you think will work best for you and your family.
2. In most communities, you can find resources and classes to assist you in or facilitate your homeschool efforts.
3. Remember, you don't have to know it all in order to effectively home education your child!

JUDY SARDEN

"We can get too easily bogged down in the academic part of homeschooling, a relatively minor part of the whole, which is to raise competent, caring, literate, happy people."

Diane Flynn Kieth

5

MAKE AN ASSESSMENT BEFORE YOU BEGIN HOMESCHOOLING

Whether you are successful in your home schooling can depend on how you set up at the beginning. It is very important to define your goals at the beginning of the school year. This means deciding how much of your curriculum you plan to cover over the course of the year, deciding whether you're going to have more academics in your school year versus more play or a mix of both. It means deciding if you're going to just focus on the things that your child is behind in or, conversely, just focus on things that your child is good at and then supplement the other areas as needed.

Deciding what is going to work best for your child and your family for the upcoming school year can be more daunting than finding curriculum. Even if you're in a state that requires certain subjects to be covered, you still have a great deal of flexibility when it comes to catering your homeschool for your child's needs and learning style.

Catching Up Academically

Some families pull their child from school because she is falling behind academically and their goal is to the child get caught up.

If this is your situation, the best advice I can give to you is to conduct your own assessment of where your child is academically. You can easily have her take a nationally normed achievement test through several vendors. Depending on her age, you can even have her take the test online.

I recommend that you conduct your own testing because if your child has been struggling academically, feedback from school officials can be extremely biased. Moreover, your child's performance could have been impacted by things that were going on in the classroom that you are unaware of. By conducting your own assessment in the comfort of your own home, you can ensure that you are receiving a more objective view of where your child is.

After you have completed your child's assessment, which you could do while he is still enrolled in school, you can then begin to set the goals for your school year. Most kids have strengths and weaknesses in different areas. By conducting the assessment, you will be able to figure out in which subjects your child needs help and in which subjects your child is performing at the appropriate level.

Remember that how your child performs on a test is not the ultimate statement as to where he is academically. Once you begin to homeschool your child, you will understand better where they stand academically. So I encourage you to simply look at your assessment as a starting point – a place to begin.

With your new assessment freshly in hand, you can now begin to select curricula, enrichment classes and co-op classes that are targeted towards bringing your child up to an appropriate academic level.

Advanced Students

On the other hand, you could be homeschooling because your child is not being challenged enough. For you, focus on how best to move your child ahead so that she is challenged at an appropriate level.

I have met many homeschooling families who pull their kids out of school because they thought that the school was not providing their children with enough challenge. If this is your situation I recommend that you also have your child independently assessed before planning out your school year. You can have your child assessed before you pull him out of school or once they are at home. Similar to the child who is falling behind, once you have your assessment in hand, you can begin to plan your curriculum and set your goals around where your student wants to go.

For a child who is academically and intellectually ahead of his peers, I strongly recommend that you involve him in the goal setting process. Advanced children will often have very strong interests or hobbies that they would like to pursue. Once you have identified your child's goals, plan your school work around helping her pursue those goals.

Also, if you find that your child is gifted in an area, you can plan around enhancing that area of advancement.

Bullied Students

If you are homeschooling because your child was in a bulling situation last year, your goal could simply be to help repair some of the damage and rebuild that child's confidence.

If you are homeschooling your child in order to get her out of a bullying situation, you'll need to keep in mind that your child has negative feelings toward anything that looks like school. Your child's self-esteem has also taken a huge hit. In these cases, it is best to look at your homeschool year as a recuperating and rebuilding time. You'll want to build in lots of successes and self-esteem building activities during this school year. So, for example, you may want to focus on finding social interactions for your child that are positive and rewarding. This doesn't necessarily mean that you have to have your child surrounded by a lot of kids. Rather, use this time to help your child find one or a few kids with whom she can build relationships.

Because of the bullying situation, your child's academic performance may have also began to suffer. If that is the case, you'll want to allow your child some time to de-school. As you'll see from Chapter 10 on de-schooling, this does not mean that you should allow your children to watch television and play video games all day. Rather, this means providing support while allowing them to pursue their education and interests. Use this time to encourage learning in a context outside of a classroom and outside of textbooks.

By allowing a child to decompress through de-schooling and by helping him to find meaningful friendships, you should be able to work your child back to where he was before the bullying began.

A word of caution. If bullying or a bad school situation has been going on for an extended period of time, do not expect your child to recover within a few weeks or even a few months. Sometimes it can take a year or two to get your child back on track socially and academically.

Medical Issues

If you are home schooling because your child has medical issues, then you will be homeschooling in an effort to keep your child on track academically while also allowing her time to attend medical appointments and recuperate.

Your goals may simply be to focus on those areas that are absolutely necessary for the academic year. I would caution you not to pressure a child who is under intensive medical care to take on too much of an academic work load. After all, the most important thing during that year is for your child to get well.

If you are debating whether to keep your child in school versus homeschooling her while she is dealing with a medical problem, I strongly recommend homeschooling. I have seen these situations with friends and the stress that a homebound child experiences while trying to get well and also keep up with the school's requirements can truly be counterproductive. A large reason for this is because schools tend to assign extra, unnecessary filler work in addition to the work that actually needs to get done. If you implement a traditional homeschool, you can ensure that your child is only doing what is necessary to complete the requirements of the school year. You can cut out the filler, you can cut out the busywork and you can cut out the extraneous activities that your child just doesn't need to deal with while focusing on getting well.

Additional Considerations

A word on academic standing. When I say that you should make sure you are doing the minimum necessary to keep up with required academic standards, please do not mistake that for meaning the only goals that you should set for your homeschool are to meet the bare minimum standards. I'm not advocating that you set the bar low and only aim to reach that low bar. I am simply pointing out that in some situations, the low bar is absolutely appropriate for starting out. As you learn and as you gain knowledge of your child, her strengths and weaknesses, and her learning style, you can always revise your goals.

Understand that you do not have to set the goal to reach the moon in order to begin homeschooling or in order to pull your child out of a bad situation at school. Know that it is okay to take things slowly, to take baby steps and that you should not become totally overwhelmed because you are trying to do everything during your first year of homeschooling or during a homeschooling reboot.

CHAPTER TAKEAWAY

1. Defining your goals and understanding what you wish to accomplish in each homeschool year will help you to decide what type of homeschool you want to implement that year and which curriculum to choose.
2. Setting goals and revisiting them often throughout the year is the best way to keep yourself accountable to your children's education.
3. Remember that your goals for your homeschool should be 100% based on your family's needs.
4. Visit www.thesardens.com/howtohomeschoolbook for a list of testing vendors.

"As regards moral courage, then, it is not so much that the public schools support it feebly, as that they suppress it firmly."

G.K. Chesterton

6

LOCATION OF YOUR HOMESCHOOL

The most exciting part of starting your homeschool journey is setting up your homeschool room. If you're like me, you spent hours looking at homeschool blogs and visiting Pinterest in an effort to come up with a design for your homeschool room. You have visions of your children sitting happily at their desks and of them diligently completing their school work.

I'm going to tell you right now to enjoy those fantasies. We have had a designated homeschool room in each of the three homes we've lived in since we began homeschooling. During the six years that I have been homeschooling, we have seldom used our homeschool room.

Instead, we homeschool all over the house, wherever it is convenient for that day. We tend to do our homeschooling wherever I am working that day. So that could be at the kitchen table, in my basemen workshop, in my bedroom, or in the lobby while I visit a customer.

You have to be sure that even after you set up your homeschool space, you allow yourself to be flexible. Don't stress out if you're not in your designated homeschool space every day.

After you figure out where your homeschool space is going to be, set up and organize your materials. We ended up purchasing some economical bookcases from the local big box discount store to store our books and other resources. I've also found that using plastic storage containers is helpful if you don't have a lot of space. Plastic storage containers can be moved under tables or in closets and out of view if you have limited space.

Decide whether you want to have posters and other educational resources affixed to the walls. This will dictate in large part where you locate your homeschool. Also decide where your children will sit. Think about where you will keep things when they are not working and also think about location and level of distraction for your children.

The beauty of setting up your homeschool space is that you can really do it anywhere! You can work outside in the yard because it's a beautiful day. If you're an outdoors person you can pack your books up and take them to the park and work under a tree. You can be anywhere while you homeschool.

The key is that regardless of how much space you have, if you figure out ahead of time where you're going to do most of your work and then organize your materials accordingly, it will take a lot of stress off of you once you begin. And again, if you start out in one place you can always change if you find that it's not working out for you.

CHAPTER TAKEAWAY

1. Have fun and be creative when setting up your homeschool location.
2. Be flexible with where you and your children decide everyone can be most productive.

"Any child who can spend an hour or two a day, or more if he wants, with adults that he likes, who are interested in the world and like to talk about it, will on most days learn far more from their talk than he would learn in a week of school."

John Holt

7

SETTING A SCHEDULE

Now that you have decided on your curriculum and set your goals, it is time to determine what your schedule is going to be. I encourage you not to feel constrained by the typical school schedule. Remember, you are homeschooling in order to maximize your child's learning and your family's flexibility.

Set a schedule, and then realize it will probably change.

I put that sentence there by itself in order to get your attention. It's okay if your schedule changes. One of the more challenging aspects to beginning your homeschool will be figuring out when everybody does their best work and then figuring out how those times work around other family commitments.

The best thing you can do for your own sanity is to set a schedule that works best with your work and sleeping schedule. For example, if you work outside the home, embrace the fact that you can homeschool at any time of day, including in the evenings and on weekends. If you or your kids are not morning people, remember that you do not have to begin lessons at 8 o'clock in the morning. You can start at 2 o'clock in the afternoon if that suits your family's needs!

Remember, too, that you can also set which days of the week you homeschool. For example, some people may homeschool three days a week, and others may homeschool five days a week, including Saturday and Sunday, because they work three days during the week.

Once you figure out which days of the week you are going to homeschool, you can now decide which hours are most convenient. For example, some people are simply not morning people. Those people will typically not begin homeschooling until noon or later. Morning people may prefer to begin their day at seven or eight o'clock in the morning. If you have implemented a traditional homeschool, as opposed to an on-line or hybrid homeschool, you will have much greater flexibility in determining what days of the week you school and which hours of the day.

When setting a schedule, keep in mind that you are not setting a schedule for a 7 ½ hour school day. That is how long most kids are in school. However, during that time they are also changing classes, sitting in homeroom, having lunch, doing specials, attending assemblies and participating in all manner of time wasting activities that schools come up with.

When you are homeschooling, you are able to cut out all these time wasting activities. Some states require a minimum amount of daily instruction. Instruction could be doing traditional, sit down at the desk academic work. Instruction can also include a field trip to the museum to discuss the latest art exhibit. It can also include hike hike up the mountain. The key is to remember that many of the activities that you do as a homeschooler will be different from the activities a child would participate in while in school.

In many states, instruction time is defined in such a way to allow the homeschooling parent flexibility in determining with that instruction time entails. Yes, you may have to cover certain subjects, but most states do not dictate how or in what manner you cover those subjects.

In a typical homeschooling setting, academic time should not take more than 4 to 5 hours a day. Here are some rough time estimates for instruction time for your children, *inclusive* of homework:

K	1-2 hours
Grade 1-2	2-3 hours
Grade 3-5	3-4 hours
Grade 6	3-4 hours
Grade 7-8	4-4.5 hour
High School	5-6 hours

As you can see, homeschooling doesn't take nearly as long as attending a brick-and-mortar school. When your children homeschool, they can complete their lessons and move on. You do not have to inflict busywork, you do not have to assign mindless numbers of worksheets, and you do not have to provide filler work to your children so that you can fill up a seven hour school day.

So when you are thinking about setting your schedule, keep in mind that homeschooling simply should not take very long.

Now, if you choose to pursue a classical based curriculum that requires significant amounts of reading, these time values can change depending on the day that you are doing the reading assignments. These time periods are average, so do keep in mind that not every day is going to look exactly the same.

Finally, I strongly recommend offering lots of short breaks between subjects, especially for younger children, so you will have to keep in mind that above are simply guidelines.

CHAPTER TAKEAWAY

1. Set your homeschool schedule in a way that causes you the least amount of stress while at the same time accommodates when your kids can be the most productive.
2. Do not become discouraged if you feel like you're not getting accomplished what you intend to get accomplished on particular day. In other words, stuff happens and if you get off track today simply get back on track tomorrow.

PART II

ADVICE AND ENCOURAGEMENT

JUDY SARDEN

"We cannot continue to send our children to Caesar for their education and be surprised when they come home as Romans."

Voddie Bauchman

JUDY SARDEN

8

YOU DO HAVE PATIENCE TO HOMESCHOOL

When I talk to people about homeschooling their children, the first response I typically get is that they do not have the patience to homeschool. This thinking is based on their current school work interactions with their children. But when you are considering homeschooling, you really have to look at school work from a different perspective.

If your child is currently in school, she's getting up early, getting breakfast, and likely catching a bus very early in the morning. She is then going to school for six to seven hours per day. By the time your child returns home from school, she has "worked" the equivalent of a full time job. If your child attends afterschool, she will have "worked" the equivalent of 10 to 12 hours for the day.

If your child is involved in any afterschool extracurricular activities, the "work day" is extended even further.

At the same time that your child was at school, you were working and going about your daily activities as well. You also have to prepare meals, complete or oversee chores, and otherwise manage and take care of household functions.

After such an exhausting day for both you and your child, it is no wonder that homework time is fraught with unhappiness, tears and other trauma. You cannot base your decision on whether to homeschool your children on how things flow during school homework time.

When you homeschool, you set your schedule based on when you and your children perform best. For many people, this means starting in the morning after breakfast. When you start at this time, you are fresh and your children are fresh. If everyone is diligent, you can get all of your academic work completed before or shortly after lunch time. At this point you will then have the rest of the day to pursue interests or simply relax.

I generally let my children sleep in, which means that we get started sometime between 8 o'clock and 9:00 AM. I am an early riser and so I typically have a couple of hours to work on my own projects before we get started for the day. Finishing early means that I then have a good part of the afternoon to continue working on my own projects.

It also gives the children time to participate in extracurricular activities and to get outside and play.

If you work outside the home, you can hire a helper to shuttle your children to activities while you work. You can facilitate lessons once you get home.

Remember, homeschooling takes a fraction of the time that children spend inside of a brick-and-mortar school everyday. This is because you do not waste any time. You do not have busywork, nor do you have to deal with any of the time wasting activities that are part of the school setting.

Adjusting Expectations

Patience is defined as one's ability to accept or tolerate delay, trouble or suffering without getting angry or upset. We all have the ability to do this.

It is also human nature to lack the capacity to exercise patience at times. No one expects you to go through life exercising the patience of Job. And while we should always thrive for patience, we should also give ourselves grace when we lose that patience.

I get annoyed and lose my patience sometimes but the kids and I get along without incident most of the time. In fact, we can go days where everything is clicking....... and then my son decides that he would rather be doing anything other than his school work. While those days can be unpleasant, they are the minority.

I've found that, after adjusting my expectations, I have the patience to deal with a child's inability to understand their assignment. At those times, I take responsibility for finding ways to present the lesson in a way that the child can understand. For example, I have learned that my younger child learns differently than my oldest and that I have to approach lessons in a way that she can understand. I often have to consult teacher's manuals and the internet to figure out how best to reach her. And that's OK because I love seeing the light turn on in her eyes when she's got it.

Before I adjusted my expectations regarding her education, I absolutely was short on patience with her.

Where I lack patience is in dealing with poor attitudes and unwillingness to try to do an assignment. But what I have found is that the poor attitude is often tied to a reluctance to admit that they need help or don't understand.

So when you are thinking about whether you have the patience to homeschool your kids, think in terms of percentages. In the course of a normal day, what percentage of impatience will you allow yourself? Twenty percent? Thirty percent? Is it enough that, over the course of a week, you were patient seventy to eighty percent of the time? And when you lost your patience, how soon afterwards were you able to get a kiss or snuggle and move on with your day? Like only a loving parent can do.

You see, that is the advantage you have when you homeschool. You can surround your children with love. Children know their parents love them. When we discipline them, most kids understand it is done in love. As parents, we can model how to deal with frustration. We can model what to say and do after we lose our temper. And we can model how to move past our frustration. These are all skills that our kids need to cope with life and are not necessarily bad. The world isn't going to be sun and roses all the time.

Managing Expectations

In my workshops, I like to discuss some common expectations that can either lead a family that wants to homeschool away from homeschooling or that can make a homeschooling family think they made the wrong decision for their family. Here I share a few of the scenarios and how, by simply adjusting one's expectations, we can move past that hurdle and be happier parents and have happier children:

My Child should be reading by kindergarten Despite the parents who will tell you that their kids taught themselves to read by age 4, most kids learn to read between ages 5 and 9. If you can accept that, your level of frustration will greatly decrease.

My child should be writing by kindergarten Some kids have fine motor skill delays and simply need time for them to develop. They should catch up by age 7, 8 or even 9.

Homeschooling should be fun The truth is, some days

are good and some are bad. You may even have a bad couple of weeks following a great 6 months when everything is falling into place. This is all normal. As in life, work and relationships with people who love us, things will get better.

I should be doing everything at home that the school is doing The great thing is that even if you live in a state that requires you to cover certain subjects, you can complete the work in a fraction of the time that the school accomplished the work. And you have the flexibility to decide *how* to cover those subjects. In most cases, only the very oldest students will have to work close to the number of hours that brick and mortar schools work.

I don't have time to cover everything We often have so many projects and plans that we overwhelm ourselves. I am totally guilty of this. Take a step back, decide what you *have* to do and then supplement where you can.

I don't think I can be around my kids all day. I NEED A BREAK!! The older your kids are, the more flexibility you have in getting away. If they can stay home by themselves, you can take a few hours to yourself. If they are littles, pop on a DVD and call it a day. The world will not end if those babies watch Little Einsteins for 2 hours! I promise. If they are in the middle grades, send them to a friend or relative's house. You can also enroll your children in co-op and enrichment classes so you have that standing time every week to recharge.

I can't get any house work done with the kids around and my house is always a mess. Welcome to the world of multiple people being around the house all day! However, all is not lost. Teach kids to pick up after themselves and have them share the housework. It shouldn't be all on you. Even the youngest children can pick up their things, wipe tables, and sort their own laundry.

CHAPTER TAKEAWAY

1. If you have the patience to hold a job, finish school, or do volunteer work, and you have the patience to home educate your children.

2. By designing your homeschool around your schedule and the needs of your family and your children, you'll find that easing into homeschooling will not be as traumatic as you anticipate.

3. Managing your expectations and allowing yourself to be flexible will greatly increase your success as you homeschool your children.

"School is about learning to wait your turn, however long it takes to come, if ever. And how to submit with a show of enthusiasm to the judgment of strangers, even if they are wrong, even if your enthusiasm is phony."

John Taylor Gatto

JUDY SARDEN

9

DON'T LET SCHOOLING GET IN THE WAY OF LEARNING

One of the things that I stress to parents, particularly new homeschooling parent, is that your goal is not to enforce a specific way of learning on a child. Yes, you do have a curriculum that you are trying to implement. Yes, you do have a schedule that you are trying to keep. Yes, you are trying to prepare your child for the future, whatever that may be. But the ultimate goal of homeschooling your child is so that he can learn and learn how to learn.

Sometimes, in our zealousness to "teach" our kids, we may find ourselves actually impeding the learning process. For example, I just had a long conversation online about learning math facts. This mom was concerned that her child was not memorizing his math facts. She was giving him timed math drills, similar to those that would be administered in a school setting. The problem was that the child was continuing to perform poorly on his timed math drills and the mom was exasperated.

You are familiar with the timed to math drills: the kid gets a sheet of, say, 50 addition or multiplication problems and they are expected to complete them in two minutes time. This child was seven years old. Now, while this mom clearly had the intention of teaching her child math facts, by forcing him to repeatedly complete the timed math drills at age 7, she was actually impeding his learning. Here's why.

As another mom pointed out, a seven year old child's inability to answer 50 problems in two minutes could largely have been an inability to actually *write* the answers as opposed to a lack of memorization. And some kids just don't learn when using a "drill and kill" process.

My daughter is an example of one of those people. Try as I might, the girl simply could not internalize her math drills. I knew that she needed to learn her math facts in order to make future math problems easier to solve. However, after harassing her for months, I realized that she simply needed me to take a different approach. I was not helping her learn; rather, I was actually standing in the way of her learning those math facts by insisting that she learn them my way.

So we moved on in math and, while periodically assigning her math facts to study, we continued on with her math as scheduled. What I found was that my daughter learned better by "doing." Meaning that as she solved problems that required recall of math facts, she learned them. I did have her continue working on math facts, but on a much less stressful and more organic fashion. And, after about 12 to 14 months, I noticed that she had automatic recall of all her math facts.

This happened within what I considered a reasonable amount of time without causing the stress, mental blocks, and self-esteem lowering activities as regards to math. We were able to achieve my goal, which was having her learn the math facts. And, at the end of the day, that's all that is important.

You will run into this type of situation over and over again when you homeschool. The key is to recognize when you're in this situation. Once you realize what the core of the problem is, it is incumbent upon *you* to figure out what changes need to be made so that your child can learn. Always remember that everyone learns differently.

I have two children and they both learn completely differently. My son was able to quickly memorize his math facts in a matter of weeks whereas it took my daughter over a year to learn the same facts.

Another thing to remember in your homeschool is that you do have flexibility. If your child has a strong interest in an area, I encourage you to do everything you can to allow him to explore that area of interest. Help your child to do everything she can to understand and get involved in that interest. Get help organizing lesson plans around the interest. What you should *not* do is simply say that, well, this area of interest does not fit within my planned curriculum and therefore we cannot cover it.

Children learn so much more and so much faster when they are doing something they want to do. In fact, it's not just children, it's adults as well. When you can incorporate learning around your child's interest, they will learn quicker, learn more, and frankly, have a better attitude about learning. And at the end of the day, isn't that what you want for your child?

I will encourage you to be flexible and think in a nontraditional way while you are homeschooling your children. Always remember that the most important thing is that they learn. How they learn what they need to learn can take many shapes and forms. And what they learn can also be very fluid. Try not to remain rigidly attached to your curriculum in lieu of allowing your child to learn.

CHAPTER TAKEAWAY

1. When homeschooling your children, keep your eyes focused on the whole child and use the opportunity to build a strong relationship with your children.
2. Remember that there is more to life than academics and be sure to explore interests and topics that fall outside of the required school subjects.

"The whole educational and professional training system is a very elaborate filter, which just weeds out people who are too independent, and who think for themselves, and who don't know how to be submissive, and so on – because they're dysfunctional to the institutions."

Noam Chomsky

JUDY SARDEN

10

DE-SCHOOLING

De-schooling is the process of helping a child, who was previously schooled in a brick-and-mortar situation, to wind down and reboot. This is accomplished in many ways. Some people choose to do nothing for a period of time. Others will choose to take lots of field trips during this time. While still others will mix some schooling in with lots of field trips and experiential learning.

De-schooling is recommended for any child who has been in a traditional school setting and who is transitioning into a homeschool setting. The reason de-schooling is recommended is because the child has learned that education means one thing and the homeschool setting typically presents a very different view of education.

Here is an example: Little Johnny is in third grade. His parents decide to remove him from school and homeschool him in the middle of the school year. Little Johnny has learned to associate "school" with lots of rules, responding to a bell, rote memorization and performing tasks in order to get a gold star, a happy face sticker, or an "A." The goal of homeschooling is to educate little Johnny in addition to teaching him independence and the love of learning. The homeschooling situation will likely look very different from the brick-and-mortar school experience. Little Johnny's parents will want to de-school him, or reset his mindset as to what school is supposed to look like.

Let's discuss how we accomplish de-schooling. As mentioned above, de-schooling can be accomplished in several ways. How you approach de-schooling will really depend on the circumstances under which you removed your child from school. For example, if you removed your child from school because of a bullying situation, your de-schooling will primarily focus on building your child's confidence and attempting to undo some of the damage that was done under the bullying situation.

If your child was removed from school because he was having difficulty academically, your de-schooling will really center around teaching him a different way to learn. For example, if your child was behind in reading, you'll want to spend time focusing on what the child is good at while gently encouraging her reading.

Example: Little Johnny was "behind" in his reading. Your de-schooling efforts will not be focused on "getting him caught up to grade level;" rather, spend time helping little Johnny discover what he's interested in. As he sets out on that journey of exploration, find written material, books and websites that help him to explore his interest. Take turns reading the material. If he is absolutely resistant to taking turns, read the material to him. Spend time outdoors, go on field trips, spend time with family. But all the while, spend time every day pursuing the things that Johnny is interested in. Little Johnny will discover that learning takes place outside of the classroom. As Johnny continues to explore what he's interested in, have him journal what he's learning.

Journaling can take many forms, including Johnny physically writing it himself, typing it, using a voice to text software, or dictating it to you.

Find ways to incorporate other subjects as you are pursuing little Johnny's interest. After you've spent several weeks de-schooling in this manner, review all that little Johnny has accomplished during this time. When little Johnny realizes how much he's learned, how enjoyable it was and how learning can be fun and relevant, you can continue on that tract, as more is of an un-schooling family, or you can then begin to ease into more structured learning.

I do believe that de-schooling should be a time of learning and of accountability. I always emphasize the fact that de-chooling should not be a time when little Johnny gets to sit and watch television and play video games for three months to get over the stress of being in school.

De-schooling should also be a time of increased responsibility at home. If homeschooling is going to take place at the child's home, this is also a time for incorporating the child in housework, meal preparation, and other tasks that have to be performed in order to keep the household running. I do not think that these are tasks for which the child should be compensated, as none of us are compensated for keeping our homes running. Keepings one's house simply means having a decent home within which to live.

All of the things that we've discussed are essentially the antithesis of being in school: exploring one's interests, learning how different subjects are relevant to what we want to do, learning life skills, and having self-directed learning. If you are planning on moving into a more structured homeschool, this de-schooling time prepares the child for more accountability, teaches him responsibility and will aid you in moving towards a more structured homeschool.

If you are not planning on doing a structured homeschool, this method is also important because it will help to ease the child into the self-directed learning necessary in an un-schooling situation.

CHAPTER TAKEAWAY

1. De-schooling is essential for a child who has been pulled out of school in the middle of the school year. This time truly allows for the child to decompress and it gives the parent a chance to ease into homeschooling in an organic way.
2. Parents should use de-schooling to really get to know their children and to understand their learning style, which will contribute towards better selection of curriculum as well as choice of homeschooling method.

"Our large schools are organized like a factory of the late 19th century: top down, command control management, a system designed to stifle creativity and independent judgment.'

David T Kearns, CEO Xerox

JUDY SARDEN

11

REALIZE MUCH OF YOUR PLANNING WILL BE IN VAIN

It can be very easy to get so caught up in homeschooling your kids that you lose sight of the fact that you have this wonderful opportunity to get to know them and enjoy them.

Similar to when the newborn infant that totally turns your life upside down. Experienced moms tell you to enjoy this time because your children are babies for such a short time. This advice might seem impossible to implement when you are sleep deprived. But then you find that the advice was correct and before you know it, your precious infant is now walking and talking and developing her own personality. And you realize that you should have cherished the time more.

When I first started homeschooling my children, I was so wrapped up in my curricula, my schedule, making sure that the children took all the right classes and attended all the best field trips. This left little time to actually enjoy the fact that I was spending so much time with them.

I would find myself so tied up with the mechanics of homeschooling that I forgot to focus on the most important aspect of homeschooling - being there for my children physically *and* emotionally, getting to know my children while they got to know me, and enjoying the wonder of experiencing their lives with them.

The beautiful thing about homeschooling is that you can organize your homeschool in such a way that works best for your family. If you find that you and your children are miserable in your homeschooling, it probably means you need to step back and make a change.

Many people find themselves throwing in the towel when everything appears to be going wrong, when in fact, all they really need to do is reorganize their homeschool in a way that works better for the family dynamic.

Another thing that may cause frustration during the homeschool is the expectation that your children will be perfectly well behaved and everything will go according to plan. Once you adjust your expectations and allow for imperfections and give yourself some grace, you will find that you'll be able to enjoy your children much more.

CHAPTER TAKEAWAY

1. I cannot over emphasize the fact that homeschooling allows you to be flexible with your child's education. If you find something is not working for you, change it!
2. Accept the fact that you do not have all the answers and that you do not know everything. Then decide where you need help and fill in the gaps where you need them. Remember, you do not have to know everything in order to homeschool your children.

"Self-education is, I firmly believe, the only kind of education there is."

Isaac Asimov

12

REMEMBER TO ENJOY YOUR CHILDREN

Before I started homeschooling my children, I was working 10 hours per day. During that time, my children were in Montessori school or in aftercare. When I began homeschooling, I enrolled my children in various enrichment classes. When I would take them to class, my son, then five years old, would insist that I remain where he could see me during the class. It seems, after leaving him for hours and hours all day every day while I worked, he did not trust me. He did not trust that I would not leave him all day again.

It took several months for my son to trust that I was going to be there. It took more months for him to begin to unload some of the unpleasant situations that he had dealt with at school. Before homeschooling, I prided myself on being open with my kids and letting them know that they couldn talk to me about anything. Indeed, even as my son was obviously going through bad times at school, he never opened up while he was in the situation; when he knew he would have to return to the school the very next day.

Now, as a young tween, my son and I have a very open flow of communication. We talk about everything. He trusts me now and I trust him.

Likewise, because we are together all day every day, I talk to my children about everything. From family finances, to my own successes and failures. Due to our proximity, we can deal with awkward social situations, hurt feelings and other growing up issues real-time.

While neither I nor my kids are perfect, and we certainly have our share of parent-child disagreements, I cherish the relationship we've been able to build while homeschooling.

Because homeschooling is not only about providing your children with an academic education. It is about teaching them about life and experiencing life with them.

As parents, it is very easy to get caught up with checking off boxes and filling in bubbles. But the privilege of homeschooling allows you to provide so much more to your children! And you can have fun while doing it.

Homeschooling parents can make a subject fun that ordinarily would not be fun. You can go on a hike through the woods just because it happens to be a beautiful day. You can play board games with your children and turn them into math lessons. You can do so many things with your children that are fun and that help build a bond that you would never have the chance to do if your children were gone to school all day.

So while you navigate how to start and run your homeschool, remember to cherish these moments that you have with your children.

CHAPTER TAKEAWAY

Remember that the time with your children is short. Do not allow the stress of planning and implementing your homeschool to take away from having fun and enjoying the time that you have with them.

JUDY SARDEN

"There is no neutral education. Education is either for domestication or for freedom."

Joao Coutinho

JUDY SARDEN

13

INCORPORATE LEARNIG INTO YOUR DAILY LIFE

When most people think about learning, they think about what goes on in school. If your children have been in school, they will likely associate learning only with being in school and studying in a book. Now that you are homeschooling, you have the opportunity to change that mindset in both your children and yourself.

Learning happens everywhere and all the time. If you don't give your children anything from your homeschooling, you should impart that bit of knowledge. Schools and academic institutions often tout how they instill in children "a love of learning." But what exactly does that mean?

In our home, it means that learning takes place everywhere we go. Learning happens at the grocery store when we are comparison shopping and looking at unit prices in order to determine where the best value is. Learning happens as I teach the children how to help me choose vegetables and plan meals.

Learning happens as we read labels together to determine whether a processed food is healthy for our bodies.

Learning happens when my children accompany me to meet with clients and when they watch how I interact with my customers. It happens as they help me price orders. In short, most of what you do in your daily life with your children encompass learning. The key is to point out what it is you would like the children to take away from a situation. You don't present it as a lesson; rather, you ask questions or start a dialog using open ended questions to see if they understood what they've seen or heard. Learning takes place in conversations that you have with your children throughout the day.

Every-day learning does not happen in the context of a written test, but rather in exposing your children to a variety of daily interactions and through many, many discussions about your experiences.

Because you'll be the one facilitating your children's learning, you'll be able to point out things in your environment that relate to what you are studying. I find that this is the best way to help solidify learning of academic material. And actually, once you get into it, it can be quite fun.

Don't worry if you think you'll never be able to do this. It will take time. But the more involved you are with your children's academics, the more you'll be able to see tie-ins in your environment.

What you'll find over time is that your children will get into the habit of seeing learning opportunities in unlikely places and will begin to lead discussions themselves. I have found this to be one of the most rewarding things about homeschooling - seeing my children make their own connections in their environment.

Another way to incorporate learning into everyday life is to look for learning opportunities when you are on vacation. No matter where you go on vacation you can always find a learning opportunity. Even if you're just spending a week at grandma's house, there is history that you can learn about the area, there are things to learn outdoors and opportunities to explore and find things that you never would have seen if you were in a "learning only happens at school" mindset.

CHAPTER TAKEAWAY

In order to instill a love of learning in your children, you will have to display a love of learning. Take advantage of learning in everyday situations. This will encourage your children to become inquisitive and to embrace a lifestyle of continuous learning.

"Self-education is the only possible education; the rest is mere veneer laid on the surface of a child's nature."

Charlotte Mason

14

WORKING WHILE HOMESCHOOLING

One of the most frequent questions that I hear from parents looking to homeschool is "how can I homeschool while working full-time?" This tends to be the biggest question for dual income homes and single parents. The good news is that you *can* still homeschool while working! It simply requires good scheduling and adequate childcare.

I want to emphasize the need to find reliable, daytime childcare for school-aged children. I live in a large metropolitan area where drop-in child care, while not common, can be found. If you do not live in an area where establishments provide this type of childcare, your next option is to find a private childcare situation. Often, neighborhood stay-at-home moms or family members will welcome the opportunity to make additional income by watching your kids.

Another option would be to hire a tutor or nanny to homeschool your children and take them to their daily activities while you work. Another option that is becoming popular is the cottage school. Many educators are beginning to homeschool their children and are offering to take in a few extra children and act as their homeschool facilitator.

In addition to childcare options, a working parent must look very carefully at the type of homeschool method they use. For example, using a hybrid homeschool may work better than doing a full time traditional homeschool.

A working homeschooling parent must also pay close attention to scheduling. You can schedule your children's homeschooling time around your work hours. If you are using an online homeschool or a boxed curriculum, your children can complete their assignments while you work and you can simply review their work when you get home.

The possibilities for what you can do as a working parent are truly endless. Obviously, the older your children are the more flexibility you have with regard to homeschooling while you are away from home working.

If you work from home, I recommend that you hire a mother's helper or part-time nanny to watch younger children while you work. If you have older children, they can generally be given assignments and allowed to check in with you only when they need help.

Following are several tips that I give to parents looking to homeschool their children while working:

- Remember That Homeschooling = Flexibility
- Find reliable, last minute child care for use when you have meetings or work-related outings
- Adapt your homeschooling schedule to your work schedule
- You don't have to school during "normal" school hours
- Focus on the work that needs to get done, rather than *when* the work is done

- Set up the longest school year that your state allows, e.g., set your school up on a 12 month calendar rather than a 9 month calendar
- Take advantage of the fact that the week is 7 days – use any of those days for school work
- Take advantage of co-ops and outside homeschool classes
- Consider on-line or hybrid schools

Set a schedule

- Once you have determined which days and times you are going to have school, set up a schedule for what gets done on each day
- Include any field trips as a school day
- Count days when you feel like you didn't get anything accomplished but you did do school. e.g., you attempted the math lesson, the kid took forever to complete the lesson or took forever and still didn't complete it. Those hours count even though you don't feel like you accomplished anything!
- Design school day around independent work vs. dependent work
- Make sure school work is age appropriate
- Remember that the younger the child, the less time you truly need for formal, academic work

Homeschooling with Littles

- Get your parent-led work done with your older student(s) during the little's nap times
- Set up "work" stations for littles, Montessori style
- School in a confined, safe area for littles to roam freely while you focus on older kids
- Take advantage of Mother's Morning Out programs in

your area for the littles to give yourself uninterrupted one on one time with older kids

CHAPTER TAKEAWAYS

1. You *can* homeschool while working, even as a single parent!
2. Working while homeschooling is all about organization and time management
3. Once you have jumped the hurdle of fixing your childcare situation, everything else should fall into place.

"The mere imparting of information is not education."

Carter G. Woodson

JUDY SARDEN

15

SOCIALIZATION

I saved this chapter for last because this is one of the easiest homeschooling issues to address. Once you start telling people that you are planning on homeschooling the first thing that they will ask you is "What about socialization?" I cringe every time someone asks me this question!

Socialization is defined as "the activity of mixing socially with others" and "the process of learning to behave in a way that is acceptable to society." Interestingly, nothing is mentioned about sitting in a classroom with 30 other children of one's same age. Nor does the definition include anything about the required location of the social activity, namely that it has to occur in a school building.

When you homeschool your children, they are with you all day every day. Parents who homeschool their children are undoubtedly teaching their children how to behave in a way that is acceptable to society. People who homeschool their children are usually also involved in many activities whether they be church, volunteer work, sports, co-op classes, enrichment classes – the list of activities is endless. Just like a baby learns to talk by listening and observing and with its parent's guidance, all children learn how to behave in society in the same manner.

Homeschooled children are no different in this regard. Everyone can give you anecdotal evidence of the homeschooled child they know who has no social skills. But for every homeschooler with no social skills, I can give you the names of at least four kids I attended high school with who meet the same criteria. Indeed, we all have attended school and worked with people who possess an utter lack of social skills, but who also went to traditional schools. My point here is that being socially awkward or an introvert is personality-based and not based upon whether a person received his education at a school building or in his own home.

In the area of socialization, homeschooled children tend to be around people of many different ages and in many different situations. For example, because my children homeschool, they spend much more time with their grandparents than they ever would have if they were in school all day every day. We travel with grandparents and my dad visits twice a week to play sports with the children. In addition to that, we have the luxury of being able to participate in volunteer opportunities at homeless shelters, the YMCA and at retirement homes that we would never be able to participate in if we only had the weekends.

My children come along with me on all of my business calls. They are with me when I am on the phone conducting household and business related conversations and they are with me as I interact with people when we run our errands during the day.

As a result, my children are quite adept at handling their own business, whether it be purchasing their own items, asking questions of sales clerks, or otherwise engaging in conversations when we are out and about.

In addition to simply living life and learning social skills that way, homeschooled children can participate in co-op and enrichment classes with other children. Homeschool groups and families can get together for play and park days every week. Homeschool families and groups can go on a field trip every day if they want. Children have the opportunity to play with their neighbors, their cousins and other family members, as well as socialize at their family's social places such as a church or health club.

You would be pretty hard pressed to find a homeschool family that literally stays at home, inside the house, all day every day. Moreover, if you look at what is going on in schools today, one has to ask if the socialization that goes on inside of a school is actually conducive to teaching a child how to behave in a way that is acceptable to society.

More and more, students are denied recess because of some minor infraction in the classroom when in fact, the last thing that student needs is to be denied the opportunity to run and play outside in fresh air. You hear of silent lunches that are implemented in order to keep down the incidence of fights. Children are trained to walk in straight lines and to follow numerous inane rules that are designed to manage classrooms. If a child to does try to "socialize" during class, she will be written up as a behavioral issue.

And so the socialization that is directed by the school does not, in my opinion, appear to be directed at the objective of allowing children to mix socially with others. And the limited amount of socialization outside of school directed socialization - that is, when students are allowed to talk and interact with each other on their own terms - seems to be counterproductive as the incidence of bullying, harassment and violence continues to escalate in schools. Indeed, with the addition of more law enforcement officers, metal detectors and other accoutrements of criminal activity detection, schools are appearing more like prisons than places of learning and "socialization."

Don't concern yourself with the notion that your children will not be "socialized" if you homeschool. As long as you are intentional about getting them out of the house and around other people, they will be fine. Notice I did not say you always need to get them around other children their age. While I am a strong believer in allowing children to play, playing with children their very same age is not necessary.

I love attending homeschool park days because I see children of all ages playing with other children of varying ages. It is not unusual to see a three-year-old running around with big kids. It's not unusual to see boys playing with girls. I love watching how our tween boys run around with their light sabers and capes because it's fun to run and play. I love watching how the homeschooled kids play with new kids when they come to join the group because the more the merrier. I love seeing, for the most part, non-cliquish behavior among the homeschooled kids. If a child misbehaves or is acting in a socially inappropriate manner, her parent is right there to correct the behavior and teach her how to properly handle herself. I chose this kind of socialization over that which is occurring in the schools.

CHAPTER TAKEAWAY

As long as you are intentional about exposing your children to many different people in many different situations, you needn't worry about whether they will be able to conduct themselves in a socially appropriate manner.

For additional content and to join my forum, visit me at www.thesardens.com!

JUDY SARDEN

ACKNOWLEDGMENTS

I would like to thank my husband, Avery, who is ever loving and ever supportive in all of my endeavors. Thank you to both my husband and my mother, who have been supportive of my desire to homeschool my children from day one. Without your support I would not have a book to write.

I would like to thank Penelope Trunk, Tom Kemnitz, and Sylvia Montoan King Wycoff for believing that I was capable of writing a book about my experiences. I especially thank Tom for his persistence in encouraging me to complete this work.

I am grateful to the support of other homeschool moms whose kindness and sharing of stories have helped me to put together the topics in this book.

And finally, I am eternally grateful to my children, who managed their assignments, played quietly with their Legos and otherwise disappeared into other rooms of the house so that I could focus on my writing.

ABOUT THE AUTHOR

JUDY SARDEN

Judy Sarden lives in Atlanta, Georgia, with her husband, two kids and one crazy cat. She practiced law for over twenty years but now spends her time focusing on homeschooling her children, writing, speaking and running a small business.

You can visit her at www.thesardens.com.

JUDY SARDEN

Made in the USA
Columbia, SC
09 April 2023